# State
# Government

*Ernestine Giesecke*

*Heinemann Library*
*Chicago, Illinois*

© 2000 Reed Educational & Professional Publishing
Published by Heinemann Library,
an imprint of Reed Educational & Professional Publishing,
Chicago, IL

Customer Service  888-454-2279
Visit our website at www.heinemannlibrary.com

Designed by Jennifer Carney
Printed in Hong Kong

04 03 02 01
10 9 8 7 6 5 4 3 2

**Library of Congress Cataloging-In-Publication Data**
Giesecke, Ernestine, 1945-
    State government / Ernestine Giesecke.
        p. cm. – (Kids' guide)
    Includes bibliographical references and index.
    Summary: Introduces the purpose and function of state government, the function of the three branches, how states raise money, how state government operates, and how a bill becomes a state law.
    ISBN 1-57572-513-4 (library)
    1. State governments—United States—Juvenile literature. [1. State governments. 2. United States—Politics and government.] I. Title. II. Series.
JK2408.G55  2000
320.473—dc21                                                        99-057609

**Acknowledgments**
The publishers would like to thank the following for permission to reproduce photographs:

AP/Wide World, pp. 5, 15, 16, 26; Massachusetts Historical Society, p. 7;  Debra Davis/Photo Edit, p. 10; Bob Daemmrich, p. 11; Michael Brosilow for Heinemann Library, p. 17; UPI-Bettmann/Corbis, p. 20; Billy Barnes/Photo Edit, p. 21; Robert Brenner/Photo Edit, p. 22; Steven Lunetta/Photo Edit, p. 23; Paul Conklin/Photo Edit, p. 24; Michelle Bridwell/Photo Edit, p. 25; A. Ramey/Photo Edit, p. 27.

Cover: AP/Wide World

The publisher would like to thank Susan Temple, of the North Carolina Department of Public Instruction, and Jay Adler for their comments in the preparation of this book.

Note to the reader: Some words are shown in bold, **like this.** You can find out what they mean by looking in the glossary.

# Contents

What Is Government? . . . . . . . . . . . . . . . . . . . . . . . .4

State Constitutions . . . . . . . . . . . . . . . . . . . . . . . .6

State Capitals . . . . . . . . . . . . . . . . . . . . . . . .8

Jobs of State Government . . . . . . . . . . . . . . . . . . .10

State Government and You . . . . . . . . . . . . . . . . . . .12

State Governors . . . . . . . . . . . . . . . . . . . . . . .14

Other State Leaders . . . . . . . . . . . . . . . . . . . . .16

State Legislatures . . . . . . . . . . . . . . . . . . . . . .18

The Judicial Branch . . . . . . . . . . . . . . . . . . . . .20

States Working Together . . . . . . . . . . . . . . . . . . .22

Money for Government . . . . . . . . . . . . . . . . . . . .24

Electing State Government . . . . . . . . . . . . . . . . . .26

How Laws Are Made . . . . . . . . . . . . . . . . . . . . .28

Finding State Government . . . . . . . . . . . . . . . . . .30

Glossary . . . . . . . . . . . . . . . . . . . . . . . .30

More Books to Read . . . . . . . . . . . . . . . . . . . . .31

Index . . . . . . . . . . . . . . . . . . . . . . . .32

# What Is Government?

**A** government is the organization of people that directs the actions of a nation, state, or community. A government has the **authority** and power to make, carry out, and **enforce** laws, and to settle disagreements about those laws.

In the United States, the government's power comes from the U.S. Constitution. The Constitution is a **document** that describes, or identifies, the powers of the government. It also places limits on those powers.

| Federal Powers | State Powers | Local Powers |
| --- | --- | --- |
| Make agreements with other nations | Vote on constitutional amendments | Make agreements with state and other local governments |
| Provide for national defense | Make agreements with other states and the national and local governments | Preserve law and order |
| Collect **taxes** on goods from other countries | Hold **elections,** decide voting requirements | Keep legal records |
| Print **currency, mint** coins | Keep powers not given to the national government | Keep powers not assigned to state or national government |

*People can band together to let state government know what is important to them.*

The main purpose of government is to carry out tasks that individuals cannot do by themselves. These include such things as protecting all the people, encouraging business so that people have jobs, and writing laws that will help people live comfortable lives.

Many nations regard protecting the rights of an individual as an important purpose of government. In the United States, the Constitution lets each person believe what he or she wishes. It gives people the right to hold meetings and express opinions—even if these opinions disagree with actions of the government.

# State Constitutions

**U**nder the **federal** system, each of the fifty states has a written constitution. Each of these constitutions describes how the state's government should be run. Each state had to have a constitution approved by the residents or their representatives before it became a state. Many states have written new constitutions since statehood.

The people who wrote each state constitution wanted to make sure that the leader, or governor, did not have too much power. So state constitutions, like the U.S. Constitution, spread power among three branches of government. Spreading the power is called **separation of powers.** This system has **checks and balances** that keep the other branches from becoming too powerful.

Vermont has the shortest state constitution — 6,600 words. Alabama has the longest — 174,000 words. The original Constitution of the United States has only 4,550 words.

**EXECUTIVE BRANCH**
**Governor**
Carries out the laws of the state

**LEGISLATIVE BRANCH**
**State Legislature**
Makes laws

**JUDICIAL BRANCH**
**State Supreme Court**
Explains laws

*After its constitution was approved, Massachusetts became the sixth state.*

Each state has an executive branch that is led by a governor. The executive branch is responsible for carrying out state laws and for carrying on the business of the state.

Each state has a legislature, which is part of the legislative branch. The people in the legislative branch are responsible for making state laws.

Massachusetts was one of the first of the states to have its state constitution approved by a vote of the people. The Massachusetts Constitution was approved in 1780.

Each state also has a judicial branch of government. This branch includes the court system, which judges actions of the government and the people in comparison to state laws.

State constitutions are much more detailed than the U.S. Constitution. They contain exact descriptions of what state **officials** may do—and how they may do it. In fact, state constitutions even tell how governments of cities and towns within the state should be set up.

# State Capitals

**E**ach state government meets in the capital city of that state. This map shows the location of each of the fifty state capitals.

Be careful not to confuse the words *capital* and *capitol.* The *capital* of a state is where the state government meets. The capital of New York is the city of Albany. A *capitol* is the main government building in a capital. The dome of the capitol in Colorado's capital, Denver, is covered in gold.

CANADA

Gulf of
St. Lawrence

*North Dakota*
Bismarck

*Minnesota*

*South Dakota*
Pierre

St. Paul

*Wisconsin*
Madison

*Michigan*
Lansing

*New Hampshire*
*Vermont*
Montpelier

*Maine*
Augusta

Concord
*Massachusetts*

Albany
Boston

*New York*
Hartford
Providence
*Rhode Island*
*Connecticut*

ne

*Nebraska*
Lincoln

*Iowa*
Des Moines

*Illinois*
Springfield

*Indiana*
Indianapolis

*Ohio*
Columbus

*Pennsylvania*
Harrisburg

Trenton
*New Jersey*

Dover
*Delaware*

Denver

*Washington, DC*
Annapolis
*Maryland*

Topeka

Jefferson City

*West
Virginia*

Richmond

*Kansas*

*Missouri*

Frankfort
Charleston

*Virginia*

*Kentucky*

Raleigh

Nashville

*North Carolina*

*Oklahoma*
Oklahoma City

*Arkansas*
Little Rock

*Tennesee*

*South
Carolina*
Columbia

Atlanta

*Mississippi*

*Alabama*

*Georgia*

*Atlantic Ocean*

Montgomery

Jackson

*Texas*

*Louisiana*

Tallahassee

Austin

Baton Rouge

*Gulf of Mexico*

*Florida*

# United States

⬕ National Capital

Seattle • State Capital

──── International Boundary

──── State Boundary

*Texas* State Name

0     400 kilometers

0     400 Miles

MEXICO

CUBA

DOM. REP.

JAMAICA

BELIZE

*Caribbean Sea*

# Jobs of State Government

State governments have many responsibilities. Much of what a state does is for the common good, meaning that it is for the benefit of all people in the state. Other jobs of the state protect peoples' individual rights.

The State Water Project in California is an example of a project for the common good. Northern California gets plenty of rain. It gets more water than is needed by people in their homes, businesses, and farms. Southern California, though, is hot and dry. Little rain falls there. However, most of California's people live in the southern part.

The California legislators decided to bring water from the north to the south in the State Water Project.

*The 444-mile (715-kilometer)-long California Aqueduct is part of the State Water Project.*

The Constitution of the United States says that laws passed by any state government may not go against any **federal** laws.

CALIFORNIA
AQUEDUCT
BRIDGE 53 2047
48 LA          10 $\frac{53}{}$

*Some states send young lawbreakers to boot camp instead of prison, so that young people can learn self-discipline and responsibility.*

States build roads and bridges to make it easier for people to do business. State programs help their farmers raise crops. States work to conserve the state's natural resources and increase the amount of business in the state. Most states try to improve their schools. States are also responsible for helping poorer people get medical help when they are sick.

State government deals with crimes such as robbery by setting up **guidelines** for the punishment a **criminal** receives. The state also keeps records of births, deaths, marriages, and divorces that take place within the state.

There is much to do. Many people work for state governments. In some states, more people work for the state government than for any business in the state.

# State Government and You

The laws of the state in which you live affect many parts of your day-to-day life.

State Government

Tests drivers before they can get a **license** to drive

Sets speed limits on many highways

Decides what training teachers need

Drivers License

Speed Limit 55

Makes up driving rules for people in the state

Watches over insurance companies to be sure they provide the services they promise

RULES OF THE ROAD

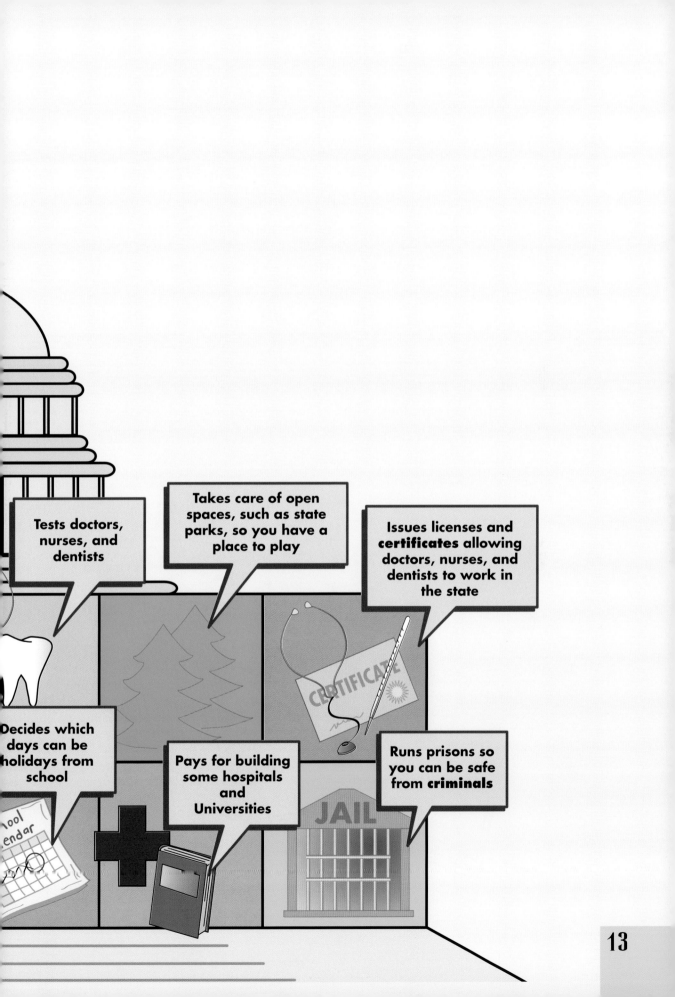

13

# State Governors

Every U.S. state has a governor elected by the people to be head of the executive branch of the state government. During his or her **term** of office—usually four years—the governor of a state lives in the governor's mansion, located in the state capital.

To be governor, a person must meet the state's constitutional requirements. In California, for example, a person needs to be eighteen years old, be a U.S. citizen, and have lived in California for five years. Other states require that the governor be at least 25 years old.

Governors take a major role in running the business of the state. They prepare the state **budget.** Once a governor prepares the budget, the state legislature votes on whether or not to accept it. In all states except North Carolina, the governor can veto, or stop, laws passed by the **legislature.**

Most governors serve a term of four years. Eight states do not allow a second term. Nineteen states allow only two terms in a row.

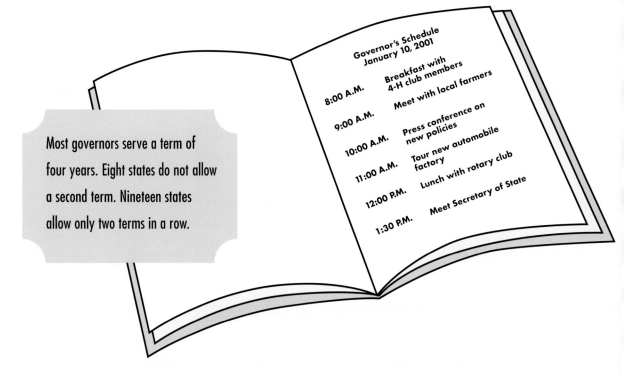

Governor's Schedule
January 10, 2001

8:00 A.M.  Breakfast with 4-H club members

9:00 A.M.  Meet with local farmers

10:00 A.M.  Press conference on new policies

11:00 A.M.  Tour new automobile factory

12:00 P.M.  Lunch with rotary club

1:30 P.M.  Meet Secretary of State

*The governor of a state is responsible for letting the legislature—and the people living in the state—know how well the state is meeting its responsibilities.*

Besides working on their own states' business, governors often work with one another. They compare how each state solves its problems. They may get together to ask the U.S. Congress for money to help states do their jobs.

Governors sometimes act as **ambassadors** representing their states. They meet with business leaders from other states or countries to encourage them to buy their states' products and to move factories to their states.

The state of Idaho often uses television—and a cartoon character named Spuddy Buddy—to advertise potatoes, the state's most important crop.

15

# Other State Leaders

The executive branch of state government includes other **officials,** too. Most states elect a lieutenant governor who helps the governor do his or her job. If the governor dies or cannot serve out his or her **term,** the lieutenant governor becomes governor.

Most states also have an elected secretary of state, but the work of these **officials** may be different. In some states, the secretary of state makes certain that **elections** are fair and honest. He or she also keeps track of official state records, including records about laws passed by the **legislature.** Often, the secretary of state is in charge of drivers' **licenses** and license plates for cars.

The attorneys general of several states worked together to show that tobacco companies were not honest with the public.

*In Illinois, the secretary of state's office is responsible for testing and licensing drivers.*

**Executive Branch**

governor
lieutenant governor
secretary of state
treasurer
**comptroller**
attorney general

Many states also choose an attorney general, the state's lawyer. He or she acts as the lawyer for all the state agencies as well as for the legislature and the governor. The attorney general protects the people of the state from things such as pollution and companies that cheat the public.

A state's educational system is usually in the hands of a person called the superintendent of public instruction, the secretary of education, or the director of education. He or she makes sure that the schools are teaching what students need to know and that school buildings and playgrounds are safe.

Most states have two people who deal with the state's money. The comptroller keeps track of the state's money and pays the state's bills. The treasurer acts as the state's banker and decides where any money not spent should be kept in order to keep it safe.

# State Legislatures

The main purpose of a state **legislature** is to pass laws. Each state's legislature can pass any law that does not go against a **federal** law or the state's own constitution.

States have different names for their legislative branch. They might be called the legislature, the general assembly, or the legislative assembly. In New Hampshire, the legislature is called the General Court.

No matter what it is called, every state's legislature—except Nebraska's—is made up of two groups, or houses. These houses are often called the State Senate and the House of Representatives or the House of Delegates. The state legislatures work in a variety of ways, but each works according to its own state's constitution.

The main work of a state legislature is to pass laws that allow the state to collect **taxes** and spend money in ways that improve the lives of the residents. Important spending programs have to do with health, education, and **welfare**.

In states with few people, the legislature may meet every other year. In most states, the legislature meets every year for about 60 days. Many legislators hold other jobs.

Most state senators are elected for four-year **terms** and representatives for two-year terms.

set the minimum age for smoking tobacco products,

encourage recycling,

require proof of **vaccinations** for students, and

require school attendance.

Legislatures also pass laws that tell which actions are crimes and how the crimes will be punished. They agree on how businesses in the state should conduct themselves. Working with both cities and the federal government, legislatures also plan highways and bridges.

Nebraska is the only state with a one-house legislature. Some people feel this arrangement avoids delays and gives voters a clear idea of who is responsible for state government.

# The Judicial Branch

The judicial branch is the third branch of state government. It is led by the state's supreme court, which explains the state's laws and makes decisions about disagreements concerning the laws. A state supreme court may have five or seven judges, called justices. In some states, these judges are elected by the people. In others, they are appointed, or chosen, by the governor.

As many as 400 other judges oversee court trials. A trial involves several people in addition to the judge. A **criminal** trial, for example, includes a defendant—the person whom the police think may have broken a law—and the defendant's lawyer. A lawyer for the state tries to prove that the defendant did something wrong. Some trials are decided by a judge, and others are decided by a group of citizens called a jury.

*A ruling by the New Jersey Supreme Court led to the day in 1984 when a girl first played in a Little League World Series.*

*In many states, the name of a child involved in a trial is kept secret. This makes it easier for the child to "start over" and keep out of trouble.*

States often have separate courts to handle special situations. Traffic courts may deal with speeding and driving under the influence of alcohol or drugs. In some states, there are special courts for people under the age of eighteen. Many states also have family courts that deal with divorces, with parents who mistreat their children, and with children who are often in trouble with the law.

Any court decision may be appealed, or reviewed, all the way to the state's supreme court or even to the United States Supreme Court. Cases that reach these top courts usually have to do with the meanings of the U.S. Constitution.

# States Working Together

States often cooperate with one another. They recognize **official documents** from one another. A birth or marriage **certificate** from Michigan is proof of identity in Wyoming. A diploma from a school in Oregon is accepted in Florida. A person who has committed a crime in one state can be arrested in a different state and sent back to the state in which the crime was committed.

States also work with one another when they share a natural feature. For example, states bordering one or more of the Great Lakes decide together how the water should be treated and how much water each state can take from the lake. The Port Authority of New York and New Jersey is a single agency in charge of the bridges and tunnels that connect the two states.

*The George Washington Bridge is part of the Port Authority. It connects New York City with the state of New Jersey.*

*The Colorado River carries millions of gallons of water as it travels
through land that is often dry and needs to be irrigated, or watered.*

Sometimes groups of states and the **federal** government work
together, especially when a valuable resource is claimed by many
states. For example, Arizona, California, Colorado, Utah, and
Wyoming all work with an office of the federal government as they
decide how to use—and how to save—the Colorado River.

# Money for Government

**M**uch of the money a state government uses comes from **taxes.** Taxes are fees paid to the government by people and companies for the privilege of living and working in the state.

Many states have taxes of various kinds. The amount of sales tax paid on purchases varies by state. In most states, the tax is a few cents for every dollar an item costs. Some states have sales tax on everything that is sold. Some states do not have a sales tax for food, medicine, or clothing. People who own property—usually land, farms, and homes—pay a tax based on what their property is worth.

At one time, California, the wealthiest state, spent $165 million a week. More than $3 million a day was spent on building and maintaining highways.

The more the property is worth, the more the person pays in taxes. Like the **federal** government, some states also use an income tax—a tax on earnings—to raise money.

*The federal government shares the costs of some roads and highways with individual states.*

*Fees for using state parks help pay for rangers to keep the park safe and maintenance to keep the park clean.*

States also raise money by charging fees to use locations owned or operated by the state. There are fees to use state parks, for example. Some states charge fees called tolls for using certain highways or bridges.

States sometimes get money from the federal government, especially for special purposes. Most federal money a state gets goes to education or assistance for poor families. Sometimes the money goes to repair highways and roads or improve public transportation.

# Electing State Government

Throughout the fifty states, the **residents** choose who will govern them. They hold **elections** and vote for the person or persons they feel will do the best job.

People who want to be elected governor or to the state **legislature** generally belong to one of two major **political parties.** Most candidates for state office belong to either the Democratic or the Republican party. There are also many smaller parties.

*State governments are made up of people chosen by the voters living in the state to be their representatives.*

*On the campaign trail, candidates might find themselves eating all kinds of interesting foods!*

**Candidates** must **campaign.** This is often called running for office. People running for office often travel through a state, meeting as many people as they can. They listen to what the voters have to say about what is right with the state and what should be changed.

There may be disagreements between people living in cities and people living in **rural** areas about what should happen in a state. It is often difficult for a person campaigning for office to please both groups of people. After thinking about the problems and possible solutions, candidates tell the voters what they plan to do if they are elected.

27

# How Laws Are Made

The idea for a law can come from a citizen or from a person already in the state's **legislature**. Either way, both the state's House and Senate must approve the idea before it becomes law.

Schoolchildren across the country have been directly responsible for some of the laws passed by their states. In Illinois, schoolchildren wanted their state to have more than a state song, a state tree, and a state flower. They wanted Illinois to have a state insect—the monarch butterfly.

One way to have the monarch butterfly named as the state insect was to have the state pass a law. This diagram shows the two ways that a bill may be introduced in order to become a law.

Sometimes the people of the state are asked to vote on the bill. This is called a referendum.

## 1

1. Schoolchildren bring the idea about a state insect to a state representative.

2. The representative writes up the idea. At this point, the idea becomes a bill.

3. The bill proposing the monarch butterfly as the state insect is presented to the state's House of Representatives.

4. A committee reads the bill and investigates the idea. They may want to know if any other state has named the monarch as their state insect. The committee reports to the whole House on the details of the bill.

5. The House votes on the bill.

6. If the bill passes the vote, it is sent to the Senate.

7. The Senate studies the bill naming the monarch butterfly as the state insect and then takes a vote.

## 2

1. Schoolchildren bring the idea of a state insect to a state senator.

2. The senator writes up the idea. At this point, the idea is called a bill.

3. The bill proposing the monarch butterfly as the state insect is presented to the state's Senate.

4. A committee reads the bill and investigates the idea. They may want to know why the children suggested one butterfly but not another. The committee reports to the whole Senate on the details of the bill.

5. The Senate votes on the bill.

6. If the bill passes the vote, it is sent to the House.

7. The House studies the bill naming the monarch butterfly as the state insect and then takes a vote.

8. If anything in the bill changes as it goes through the process, a committee of representatives and senators work out the final wording of the bill.

9. The House and the Senate vote on the bill. If the bill passes the vote, it is sent to the governor to sign.

10. The governor signs the bill and it becomes a law. By law, the monarch butterfly becomes the state insect.

# Finding State Government

One way you can take part in state government is to write your state representative or senator. You can ask for information about the plans he or she has for education or for saving the environment. Find out which bills your representative or senator supports. Let him or her know which bills you think are not very good ideas.

Your local telephone book may list the names of your state senators and representatives. A local librarian can also help you find out where to write, or you can find information from your state's website on the Internet. Ask your librarian to help you find the home page for your state.

# Glossary

**ambassador** messenger or representative

**authority** power to enforce laws, command obedience, or judge

**budget** plan describing the amount of money that will be spent and received during a given time

**campaign** organized effort to win election to public office

**candidate** person who wants to be elected to a public office

**certificate** written proof of birth, or proof of the ability needed to practice a certain profession

**checks and balances** system that makes sure different parts of government cannot become stronger than other parts

**comptroller** person who keeps track of money that is taken in or spent

**criminal** having to do with crime, such as robbery; a person who commits a crime

**currency** paper money or coins that are used in a country

**document** written or printed paper

**election** process of making a choice by voting

**enforce** to make people obey

**federal** referring to a group of states that give up some power to a central government, also referring to the central government of the United States

**guideline** statement of rules to follow

**legislature** group of people with power to make or change a state's laws

**license** paper that shows that someone is allowed to do something, such as teach school, drive a car, or practice medicine

**mint** to manufacture coins

**official** elected or appointed person in a position of power, also refers to any item that is recognized as being legal

**political party** group of people who have similar views about government

**resident** person who lives in a state for at least a minimum period of time that is set by state law

**rural** areas that are in the country

**separation of powers** system of government that distributes power among several branches and keeps each branch separate by making it illegal for persons serving in one branch to serve in another

**tax** money required by the government for its support; may be based on property owned, money earned, or things bought

**term** length of time, set by law, served by an elected person

**vaccination** medicine given to protect against certain diseases

**welfare** providing money, health care, food, or housing for those who can't afford it

# More Books to Read

Feinberg, Barbara. *State Governments*. New York: Franklin Watts, Inc., 1993.

Heath, David. *Elections in the United States*. Minneapolis: Capstone Press, Inc., 1998.

Womack, Randy L., and James L. Shoemaker. *The Complete Book of U.S. State Studies*. Redding, Cal.: Golden Educational Center, 1996.

# Index

Alabama  6

attorney general  16, 17

bill, becomes law  28, 29, 30

birth certificates  22

California  10, 14, 23, 24

campaign  27

candidate  26, 27

certificates  13, 22

Colorado  8, 23

common good  10

comptroller  17

constitution
   state  6, 7, 14, 18
   United States  4, 5, 6, 7, 10, 21

courts  6, 7, 20, 21

defendant  20

director of education  17

elections  4, 16, 26

executive branch  6, 7, 14, 16, 17

federal government  19, 23, 24, 25

federal system of
   government  6

governor  6, 7, 14, 15, 16, 17, 20, 26, 29

houses  18, 19

Idaho  15

Illinois  28, 29

judge  20

judicial branch  6, 7, 20

jury  20

laws  4, 5, 6, 7, 10, 12, 14, 16, 18, 19,
   20, 21
   how they are made  28, 29

legislative branch  6, 7, 18

legislator  10, 18

licenses  16

lieutenant governor  16, 17

Massachusetts  7

Nebraska  18, 19

New Jersey  20, 22

New York  8, 22

North Carolina  14

political party  26

representative  6, 18

responsibilities, state  7, 10, 11

rights  5, 10

schools  11, 17, 22

secretary of state  16, 17

state capitals (map)  8–9

superintendent of public instruction  17

supreme court  6, 20, 21

tax  4, 18, 24
   income tax  24
   property tax  24
   sales tax  24

treasurer  17

Vermont  6